Reflections of my Family Treasures: Memories of Healing Hearts Built Upon Love, Thanksgiving and Forgiveness Between Siblings

By Theresa A. Jones

BLCKSEEDSPUBLISHING.
PLANTING SEEDS OF LOVE, FORGIVENESS & HEALING

-Reflections of My Family Treasures-

Copyright © 2023 by Theresa A. Jones

All rights reserved. No part of this publication may be reproduced, distributed, or transmitted in any form or by any means, including photocopying, recording, or other electronic or mechanical methods, without the prior written permission of the publisher, except in the case of brief quotations embodied in critical reviews and certain other noncommercial uses permitted by copyright law. For permission requests, write to the publisher at the address below.

Black Seeds Publishing
support@blackseedspublishing.com
www.blackseedspublishing.com

The views expressed in this publication are those of the author and do not necessarily reflect the official policy or position of any other agency, organization, employer or company associated with the publisher.

Scripture quotations taken from the Holy Bible, King James Version, unless otherwise noted.

Ordering Information:
Quantity sales. Special discounts are available on quantity purchases by corporations, associations, and others. For details, contact the publisher at the address above.

-Reflections of My Family Treasures-

Printed in the United States of America

ISBN-13: 979-8-9878956-9-6

BL✿**CKSEEDSPUBLISHING.**
PLANTING SEEDS OF LOVE, FORGIVENESS & HEALING

-Reflections of My Family Treasures-

"FORGIVENESS IS NOT AN OCCASIONAL ACT; IT IS A CONSTANT ATTITUDE".

-DR. MARTIN LUTHER KING, JR.

BLACKSEEDSPUBLISHING.
PLANTING SEEDS OF LOVE, FORGIVENESS & HEALING

-Reflections of My Family Treasures-

Dedication

To Naomi McNair, my mother who taught us how to love and care for each other. August 3, 1937-January 16, 2012.

James Myers Jr. My Oldest sibling and brother, I learned to respect in love with forgiveness and thanksgiving. September 29, 1954 -January 20, 2022.

−Reflections of My Family Treasures−

Table of Contents

Dedication v

Foreword viii

Introduction 1

Chapter 1: Summer Breeze and Bottle Milk 5

Chapter 2: Moving Forward 11

Chapter 3: Silly Stuff, Hard Knocks and Pains 17

Chapter 4: Theresa on the Lookout 23

Chapter 5: Onward and Upward 26

Chapter 6: A Prayer Reminder 34

Chapter 7: Big Brother Jimmy 37

Chapter 8: Fed Up and Tired 40

Chapter 9: A Welcomed Addition 44

Chapter 10: Then Came Keith 48

Chapter 11: Life in the Big House 52

Chapter 12: A New Attitude 55

Chapter 13: Rise and Shine 59

Chapter 14: Reaping and Facing the Music 62

-Reflections of My Family Treasures-

Chapter 15: Final Hurrah...66
Chapter 16: Kudos to You Mom..70
Special Tribute to Siblings...75
About the Author..82
Acknowledgements..85

Foreword

By Tiffany A. Hardison, Friend and Confidant

Psalm 118:24 declares, "This is the day which the Lord hath made; we will rejoice and be glad in it." These words are positively expressed everyday from this amazing author. And she does just that, while encouraging others to do the same! What a beautiful way to start the day.

I have been blessed to be a witness of this woman's journey. And I am truly proud. You will experience the genuine love from her heart as you read each page.

She truly lives the life that she speaks about. It's quite an honor to know someone so dedicated to uplifting others and will always leave you with a heartfelt "God Bless You".

I'm very excited that we all get to read these words of love. I know that 'Reflections of My Family Treasures' will be filled with lessons and blessings we can apply.

For as long as I've known her, she's been an amazing writer, fluent poet, an uplifting speaker, the best supporter one could ever have, and simply an all around beautiful Woman of God.

-Reflections of My Family Treasures-

This loving author is my mother, my sweet girl, my friend and I love her to life. She has been shining the light of love to so many for so long. And now she's blessing the world by doing so as a magnificent author.

Tiffany A. Hardison

-Reflections of My Family Treasures-

OUR SHARED MEMORIES AND EXPERIENCES STRENGTHEN OUR SIBLING CONNECTION.

-AFFIRM

BLCKSEEDSPUBLISHING.
PLANTING SEEDS OF LOVE, FORGIVENESS & HEALING

REFLECTIONS OF MY FAMILY TREASURES: MEMORIES OF HEALING HEARTS BUILT UPON LOVE, THANKSGIVING AND FORGIVENESS BETWEEN SIBLINGS

BL¥CKSEEDSPUBLISHING.
PLANTING SEEDS OF LOVE, FORGIVENESS & HEALING

Introduction

Before I formed thee, I knew thee.
Jeremiah1:4 (KJV)

As a child, I understood that Sunday was a time to commune with God. We spent time in the house of the Lord, learned Sunday school lessons, and learned how to respect God's house.

When Mama and Grandma told us to be still and listen, they meant it. It took a lot of smacks and pinches in the pews for me to get the picture.

I loved the music and that was my prime reason for church and the height of service for me. I can still hear the old sounds of 'Amazing Grace' and 'Jesus Paid It All'. The old Shiloh Baptist Church was just a hop, skip and a jump down the street from where we lived. During the week, Mother would walk around the house singing with the most heavenly voice. I would think to myself, "Sing Mom, sing."

She loved Mahalia Jackson and Shirley Caesar. Although I didn't always understand the message, the sound of something good drew me in. My ears would pick up moms humming no matter where she was in the house, and I would go to meet it. I stuck to Mom like glue on most occasions, even when she didn't know I was there. The presence of God in her was touching my life.

The scripture speaks about train up a child while they are young, and when they are old, they won't depart. Many a day during my adolescent years I would hear my mother's voice saying: Stop, No, Don't and Wait. The loving authority in which I heard her would stir me to do the right thing. She would teach us to love one another. Apologize when we had done wrong. She elaborated on how forgiving and being forgiven was a mighty healing of freedom.

A mother is a precious gift, a treasure for all time. I am thankful for the well-spoken advice my loved one gave before her passing in January 2012. Someone once said that you only get one mother. Truly I thank God for mine.

You see it's the things she said while yet living that leave such an impression on us, even now as she's gone. We remember the instructions and directions she tried to instill in us. Even now I can still hear her saying, always love, forgive and be thankful for one another and the gift God has given you. In doing so, you will instill within a healthy, happy, successful life of healing and everyday freedom.

To follow one's advice through life, you have to really hear what their saying, get an understanding, and trust it. Mother indeed was a jewel, a precious pearl and treasure.

As adults, we now teach our own children and grandchildren the lessons of healing and forgiveness that we were taught.

Thank you Mom 🙏

My Mom

-Reflections of My Family Treasures-

SIBLING LOVE IS A CONSTANT SOURCE OF JOY AND SUPPORT IN MY LIFE.
-AFFIRM

BLCKSEEDSPUBLISHING.
PLANTING SEEDS OF LOVE, FORGIVENESS & HEALING

-Reflections of My Family Treasures-

Chapter 1: Summer Breeze and Bottle Milk

My mother's story, which I've written as best as my memory serves me from the age of three, might even be your life narrative.

Scripture records it like this:

> "The thing that hath been, it is that which shall be; and that which is done is that which shall be done: and there is no new thing under the sun." -Ecclesiastes 1:9 (KJV).

I was born in the late 1950s. Later in life, I would come to know this on my own through life experience, phrases, words, styles, hairdos, and clothing... that which I thought was a new style had been worn or created years before my time.

In the 70's, I had a pair of silver glittery platform shoes that I wore on my wedding day. Can you imagine the look on my face when I found out that those platform shoes had been on the market for years?

– Reflections of My Family Treasures –

I bought my husband a butterfly shirt because I loved those collars. I thought the look was fresh and new. It was for me. As handsome as it looked on him, I found out that if you saw an episode of Bonanza from back in the 50's, you would see the Cartwrights wardrobe was full of them. I guess it wasn't new after all.

In the course of one's life, if you live long enough, you will see very similar, if not the same, waves being processed again, such as the beehive's hairstyle. There truly is nothing new under the sun (Ecclesiastes 1:9).

Moving forward, life began to take shape, as my memory would hold all of life's happenings from age 3 on. Though many were not pleasant, my determination would be to get to age 4; life had to be greater than now. My beautiful mother would see us through.

❦

We grew up in a section with uphill lawns full of grass in an area known as Minersville in Cambria City, Johnstown, Pennsylvania. Our apartment was over a convenience store.

My one joy was riding my bouncing horse. I remember long hours bouncing and looking toward the sky while sucking on my popsicle. I was content.

The neighbors would park all kinds of weird ways to get to the store. The sounds of porch doors creaking as they opened or slamming closed as people entered or exited their homes were everyday activities that I listened to.

The warm breeze caressing the side of my face close to the sun felt pleasant. Not knowing the meaning of friendship then, looking back, I would say, I had one friend... it was the sun.

I didn't like the cold. Mother and Father had four of us at the time. Two of Mother's seeds, she would later tell us, didn't make it. Larry was born with an ailment and died at two, while baby Myers was stillborn. There would have been seven boys and only two girls. But as God would have it, Mother healed and moved on to take care of her living children.

One of my fondest memories is watching my mother make the twins' formula. She would put Karo syrup in their milk, and I asked why. She said, "It has a sweet taste, and they drink all of it." My oh my, knowledge to my ears!

The moment the twins went to sleep, I tasted the formula. It was so good. From that time forward, I would sip more bottled milk than they did and save them some. Looking back, I should have been ashamed of myself. I was 3 years older.

Our apartment wasn't very big, so there were many days when I felt like I was being deprived of the formula. I had to wait until my mother was in another room for long periods of time to be sure she wouldn't catch me drinking the twins' milk. I didn't know anything about addiction then, but I had become hooked on formula.

From the first taste, all I wanted was more. Mother couldn't understand how they were drinking so much. They cried a lot because they were hungry. Mother would say, "You can't be hungry because I just fed you. The whole bottle is gone."

She assumed their diapers must be wet. "Nope, they're not wet," I would hear her say. I would slip out of the back door and get on my bouncy horse, looking up at the sun and enjoying its warmth, wondering when the opportunity would present itself to get some more of that formula.

At the age of 3, I was old enough to know right from wrong; however, I would come to know in later years what the scripture meant: What's done in the dark will come to light... specifically, Luke 12:2-3:

> ....
> 2For there is nothing covered, that shall not be revealed; neither hid, that shall not be known.
> ....

> [3] Therefore whatsoever ye have spoken in darkness shall be heard in the light; and that which ye have spoken in the ear in closets shall be proclaimed upon the housetops.

Busted and caught by Mom with a bottle in hand, I headed back, enjoying myself while one of the twins cried. After my spanking, I would come to know that my backside was burning. I was addicted.

Mother kept preaching the spare the rod, spoil the child scripture about love and discipline (Proverbs 13:24), except she said it like this: A hard head makes a soft behind. She said what she meant, and she meant what she said. I finally got the message.

For as much as I knew then, our family was great together until I started being startled awake from my naps by loud yelling. The yelling would continue for what felt like hours, leaving me feeling anxious and on edge. I couldn't understand why our once peaceful family dynamic had suddenly shifted.

WE UPLIFT AND INSPIRE EACH OTHER TO REACH OUR HIGHEST POTENTIAL.

-AFFIRM

Chapter 2: Moving Forward

I guess one could say that everyone looks at their mother and thinks, "WOW, Mom sure is pretty!" And that was my thought exactly about my mother.

With long beautiful Indian-like hair, fair complexion, and green colored hazel eyes, she was gorgeous. She shared with us that as a young girl, her hair was in long ponytails. The desks at school had ink wells and the boys that sat behind her in class would put the end of her hair in the ink. 'Boys will be boys,' I thought.

She loved to sing the gospel songs by Pastor Shirley Caesar and Mahalia Jackson. 'No Charge' and 'How I Got Over' were two of her favorites. She seemed to have so much joy with authority every day, until the clock struck 6:00 p.m. the mood of the house would change. I knew Dad had come home.

Before payday, it always seemed like voices got louder and louder. Mother and Father had their own struggles to work out. The words and actions I saw and heard brought tears to my eyes. At three years of age, I detected some things I just didn't want to know about. However, I began to see things no child wants to notice between her parents. I gathered from Mom and Dad's glaring looks rattled emotions flying arms and loud voices that our happy home wasn't so happy.

Things were not well. One evening as this kind of behavior was becoming a habit, I saw hands swinging and Mom on the floor. My hero. I guess every girl wants to come to her mother's rescue. Before I knew it I had grabbed a small steak knife, telling him to get out or I would hurt him. Dad left the house.

The next thing I knew, after that incident, we moved from the first home I'd known in Minersville to Kernville on Menoher Boulevard. Mother would later tell me in life, that when she heard me say those words to Dad, she knew she had stayed too long and it was time to go.

Few things in life about a troubled marriage are funny, very few. As I grew older hearing my mother describe how I grabbed that dull steak knife, 25 pounds of sternness facing a giant without fear brought a chuckle from within. I didn't know it then, but life's challenges would be numerous in my life and I'd find an inner strength to face them all with a savior I had yet to know.

Many days as I met other young people in the neighborhood, I found that Mom wasn't the only single parent and us without a father figure. I wondered if this was the norm or if God had other plans for my family.

New Ground and Rules

Today's a brand new day, new house new neighborhood new neighbors, and of course, new rules. 'Stay away from strangers.' Well, in our case a stranger was everybody until Mom got to know you.

One rule was always sure—no playing ball in the house. Even if it was a small ball and we rolled it across the floor, eventually we'd raise to our knees and start playing catch. The next thing we knew, something would be breaking.

But the newest rule for this area was to 'Watch', because we now lived on a highway where many cars traveled fast. We didn't have much of a backyard. It was at this new house that many hardships would come my way, and they kept coming year after year.

'Stay out of the street. Don't go near the curb, and be careful of playing on the sidewalk.'

I thought, "Don't do this, don't do that. Don't open the door when I'm not home." But the hard knocks life was just about to start.

"Listen carefully to me," she would say, "and pay attention." Then would come the test, "Now, what did I say?"

Jimmy and I were the accountable ones as the twins were so young. Our only response was, "Don't' play ball in the house." Then she'd repeat all of the rules that we didn't respond to. The lesson we learned from that was to make sure we listened the first time around, so we wouldn't have to hear it again.

We had a great Aunt that lived across the street and helped keep an eye out for us. We were under a microscope, as she watched every movement. As children, we did what kids do, but never got by. "Hey, did your momma tell you to open that door? You better get back in that house!" She would yell out from her house at us.

On a second attempt, we came out to a shaking finger. We gave up because we knew we had caused trouble upon us because great Auntie would tell, and she did.

Mom met our neighbors that lived upstairs, The Brooks, the nicest people ever. They were a bit younger than great Auntie and became Mom's extra helpers.

We loved them but when our plans of getting outside failed, we did the one thing we shouldn't have, grabbed a ball and broke rule #1. It was all good until one of us hit the ball so hard that it bounced right into Mom's beautiful lamp. We scurried to clean up the glass, but had nowhere to hang the lampshade. Now we'd get it for sure!

Mom's big question, "Who broke my lamp?"

Jimmy said, "Theresa." And I said, "Jimmy."

And then the even bigger question, Mom asked, "Were you all playing ball in here?"

How do moms always know? The punishment wasn't worth it. The whooping we got with an old extension cord hurt. I cried for him and he cried for me as we promised never to play ball in the house ever again.

We gave each other a big old hug, apologizing to one another. As the twins woke up seeing us crying and jumping, trying to miss Mom's aims, it was funny to them. I can still see them pointing and laughing. The older siblings had learned a valuable lesson that day and sealed it with love.

THROUGH THICK AND THIN, MY SIBLINGS AND I STAND TOGETHER AS A UNITED FRONT.

-AFFIRM

Chapter 3: Silly Stuff, Hard Knocks and Pains

The outside rules were understandable, however, though one or two may have occurred, it was in the house that I got in the most trouble. My fascination with watching my mother wring out clothes in our old-fashioned washing machine often got my attention.

I couldn't wait to put something through the wringer myself. Watching the water being squeezed out seemed fun, however, one day trying it on my own wasn't a fun experience and I created a not-so-fun situation for myself.

Clothes always seemed easily wrung out. I got the bright idea of putting my doll baby's shoe through, however, it went in so fast followed by my left hand's fingers and then my skinny little arm. Frightened, I used my right hand to try and pull myself loose.

"Oh boy," I thought, "I'm in trouble now."

As I was lifted up off the floor, I began screaming for Mother, who hurried down the steps and gave the machine a whack that set me free. Mom saved me, my beautiful hero, "Thank you, Mom," I praised as I was rushed to the hospital. I was treated for my bruises and released—not knowing it would be one of many visitations.

❦

So as life would have it, there was a day when I wanted to be the first to take a bath. In our new home was the most beautiful oval-shaped tub, the prettiest color of blue. All I'd ever known was the old white tub. First, that's when the water was the hottest. If you were second in line, you had to wait another hour for the water to heat back up.

I always made it as hot as I could. I never liked anything lukewarm. Even as I write this now, I'm reminded of the passage in the bible where Jesus declares about us being hot or cold, lukewarm he will spew us out of his mouth (Revelations 3:16).

❦

On a particular day, my oldest brother was trying to sneak into the bathroom. Catching a glimpse of him out of the corner of my eye, I yelled, "That's my bath!" We began to wrestle trying to keep each other from being first in my bathwater, and then I fell into that hot tub of water. Screams permeated the room as the pain shot through my body.

My brother ran out of the bathroom finally, while Mother ran in, helping me out of that tub, out of those hot drenched clothes. Wrapping me in sheets, I was rushed again to the hospital.

I had to lay on my stomach for weeks as they had bandaged my bottom pretty well. My goodness, soup and Jello always. Why, I wondered, is that the recommended meal for every catastrophe?

Boy oh boy, children's ward again. Watching the other children up and about made me sad as I couldn't participate in any activities. Right then and there I made up my mind that I was done with hospitals.

Dismissal day couldn't come soon enough. After three days in the hospital, I went home, still having to lie on my stomach, but this time in my own bed.

Summer was passing by. I wanted to enjoy some of it outside. Many days I would be mad at my brother and relive the bathtub scene again, and think, 'but it was my bathwater.'

It was times like these that I could hear Mom say, "Don't fight each other, Jimmy protect your younger siblings, and have respect for the oldest sibling. Always love and forgive one another to maintain continuous healing and freedom in your heart."

Pressing On

Some things stick in your mind, and you become determined that you will not be in the caseload spoken about your future. After that third trip to the hospital, my nurse simply said, "We'll just keep a room for you, Theresa you'll be back."

My incidents, or perhaps I'll call them mishaps, were becoming a habit I didn't like, especially when a place of permanency was being added to it. One episode mainly because of curiosity led me to an act of doing what my mother said never to do—that was the washing machine event.

I had no idea that the baby doll shoe would be snatched so quickly. I still carry the visible scars where the skin was stretched on my lower and upper left arm as I tried to free myself with my right hand. What a reminder of listening to Mother. The bathtub incident also left reminders on my lower back. I determined within myself, that I would not be going back to the children's ward any time soon, and that I'd be more careful.

❦

I took extra precautions watching, looking both ways before crossing streets, and thinking before reacting.

― Reflections of My Family Treasures ―

Growing up became a chore. I had to watch out for myself, and that became a full-time job.

I needed some help and realized that my habitual prayer of, 'Lord lay me down to sleep, I pray the Lord my soul to keep, if I should die before I wake, I pray the Lord my soul to take' was good, however, I felt in my heart that I needed a greater keeper.

Asking God to help me became real. Every time I stepped out of the house to go up or down the street, I would look up at the sky and say, "Be with me, God." I meant it.

I had seen Mother so many times on bended knee praying to God. I followed her lead. I knew I wasn't accident-prone, however, my not listening caused many a stir.

I remember being about 10 years old. I was excited about the double digits I had reached. I made it. My prayers were being answered. My accidents became less and less. Thank you, Lord.

OUR DIFFERENCES ONLY ADD TO THE RICHNESS OF OUR SIBLING RELATIONSHIP.

-AFFIRM

Chapter 4: Theresa on the Lookout

As life would have it, all work and no play was making me a very dull girl. Mother's sister my Aunt Fannie was coming over for a visit. Her family lived close by in the neighborhood.

While playing a game of tag, I pushed my cousin Randy and took off running down the alley right smack into a big black jalopy, which thankfully was just creeping along—an insurance man who knew to drive slow because of the neighborhood children in the area.

I had much spunk as they say back in the day. Determined not to let cousin Randy catch me, I jumped up and kept running. The report got back to Mother that I had gotten hit by a car. While the insurance man, the family and neighbors were frantic in trying to find me, I had run up another alley and down the street to my house and went in.

My right jaw had swollen up like a cantaloupe. I was rushed to the hospital once again to be treated, I can remember a nurse saying, "Theresa, what are we going to do with you?"

All I know is being hit by that car made me not want to go outside for awhile, especially running down alleys. House bound again for a few days, I planned a way of escape for myself to be more careful outside, looking to the right and left while stopping at the stop signs. This would take some discipline.

As an adult now, I realize that my mind has always been fast. My training in school for spelling competitions, athletic track and field, even playing hide and seek along with dodge ball caused me to move quickly. Now paying attention to my surroundings, looking twice before crossing a street are the safe things I look for.

Days later when we saw each other, Randy said, "Cousin I'm glad you're okay, and I'm sorry you got hit, but glad you home now." We hugged and then he said, "Oh yeah, you're it!" then ran outside. I smiled, glad to be safe in the house.

Remembering our apology to one another, Randy and I went our separate ways. Years later at a family gathering the game goes on as I see Randy and say, "Hey cuz how have you been?" Before he could answer, I said, "Guess what, you're it!" We laughed and hugged. The joy of family love remained among us.

I CHERISH THE LAUGHTER, THE TEARS, AND EVERY MOMENT WE'VE SHARED.

-AFFIRM

BLCKSEEDSPUBLISHING.
PLANTING SEEDS OF LOVE, FORGIVENESS & HEALING

Chapter 5: Onward and Upward

Mother told us that our house was a shelter for a time. We knew we wouldn't be there long and it was no surprise after a few years when she announced that she had found a bigger house. I didn't really care because too much had happened to me while we lived in Kernville.

Mother talked about it being a blessing in her time of need. She found a much larger house with three bedrooms. I was fine with that after all the incidents and accidents that had happened to me in that house, a fresh start would be welcomed.

We moved to Strauss Avenue, our next residence about two blocks up and around the corner. It was there where I found my first friends, in a new neighborhood two doors down from our new home.

Linda and Loretta were known as 'PK's' (preacher's kids). They had a house full of boys and just the two girls. Their father, Reverend Matthew Sr. played the piano and sang. His favorite song dear to my heart was 'When All God's Children Get Together'.

I spent many days there listening to gospel music and anticipating the wonderful meals their mother so eloquently made. Her specialty was pineapple upside-down cake, scrumptious!

I developed a second home and my mom was okay with it. It was there with the gospel music and singing around the piano, that an increase of growth and change began to come. My insides were stirred, my mindset opened up and my heart began to treasure all the newness of life I'd begun experiencing.

I didn't want to miss anything happening in this fresh lane of life, so I grabbed a piece of paper and began to write the joys of my day's events. I was twelve.

❦

Another joy I soon discovered, I loved to write. Words came easily to me, increasing my vocabulary. Words of rhyme, patterns of rhythm, sentences of excitement, paragraphs of completion, I was thrilled that what I was saying was something wonderful. I realized God had given me a gift to write and not just a gift of gab.

I was blessed to know this family. I loved them and they loved me. My mom, a good judge of character, allowed me to fellowship on Sundays. Reverend Tisinger pastored the Beulah Baptist Church in Indiana, Pennsylvania.

−Reflections of My Family Treasures−

I had so much fun there. I began thanking God so much for opening this door to meet this great family. What awesome treasures and gifts He had given to me.

Then one day in Sunday school, I heard this scripture, 1 Thessalonians 5:18:

> In every thing give thanks: for this is the will of God in Christ Jesus concerning you.

Knowing the application of the Word had been put in my path, I smiled as I yet did not know Jesus as Lord—but He knew me. I thanked Mom for leasing me to this family. I thanked God for them receiving me. I thanked God for my recognition of the writing gift ability. For James 1:17 says:

> Every good gift and every perfect gift is from above, and cometh down from the Father of lights, with whom is no variableness, neither shadow of turning.

As life would have it, good fortune had come our way. My grandmother, who lived a block away, bought some properties in the Kernville area where we lived. She offered the home to Mom for payment of $1. Can you believe that?!

Of course, Mother accepted the offer and we were back on Menoher Boulevard, two houses up from where we had lived before moving to Strauss Avenue.

🍀

We left Menoher with myself and three brothers, however; we now had a fifth child. She could have been mine as far as I was concerned. I wanted a sister and truly without knowing any other prayer than the Lord's prayer, I cried out, "Lord help my mommy have a girl, a sister for me."

Wow, on March 3, 1965, on a blistery winter day, my prayer had come to pass. Mom named her Lisa Michelle. She was fair complexioned and had rosy cheeks. In a word, she was beautiful. I remember singing over and over again, "I got me a sister, I got me a sister!"

What a special treasure. Better than any piece of gold or silver was this lovely bundle of joy. Jimmy, Fred, and Derrick were getting sick of my cherry attitude and gave me looks that said, "So." But I was a happy camper. All I could say was thank you, God.

Mom explained how the new house would need much work so it was weeks before we even saw our new home for the first time; and as soon as I saw it, I noticed how huge and old it looked. Our new home did need much work so Mother and her helpers continued to get it in good shape before we would see it again.

After a few weeks, we went for the second time. I noticed how much had been done, and still needed to be done. My eyes could not see their master plan, and yet they had one. Mother assured us that we wouldn't believe our eyes within one month. She was right! We finally moved into the big house, a place I'd known as home throughout my teenage years.

❦

It's now 1970, and June is just around the corner. I'm planning on what I wanted to do for my 13th birthday. I got a card and cake. The family sang the Happy Birthday song and life moved on.

Mother and my stepfather, Jay, were now planning their wedding. As they worked and labored on the house the weeks turned to months, and the months into years. She and Jay were like master builders working together for a purpose. They wanted the house completed before they were married, but took a break to say I do.

The wedding day arrived. He and Mother were married on April 27, 1971. So beautiful, her favorite color was yellow. I can still see her walking down the stairs of the house on the way to the church.

Jay in his yellow tuxedo jacket was indeed a handsome man. His smile defined him in a word gorgeous. The wedding party consisted of her bridesmaid cousin Gladys, her maid of honor sister Aunt Fannie, Jimmy would give Mom away as Tim would be the ring boy and Lisa the flower girl. Our stepbrother Bruce was Jay's best man. What a day to remember.

There was a time when I thought Mom and I were doing fine without her remarrying. But together there was so much joy. I had put my selfishness aside, asking God to forgive me for the thought, as it wasn't one of the loving traits she had taught us.

I remember their joy as they stood side by side in the kitchen while cooking dinner. Mom could, as they say burn—meaning get down with it. Jay was a true chef and the food with their skill of seasoning was magnificent.

One of our favorite meals was stir fry and rice. I loved going to the market with Mom to shop except she took too long. Mother shopped in the meat department like most women do for shoes. She took her time checking the price, lean of meat, and expiration date. If too much fat it goes back on the shelf.

Mother taught us to get our meats worth for our buck. "Check the dates," she'd say. The thought she put into every detail was significant to the love respect and thanksgiving she had for her family. She always gave us her best and taught us to do the very same for one another.

In every aspect, it seemed that Mom was teaching a lesson. I was trying to grasp all she was saying. The house was thriving, a place I was proud to call home and bring friends to. Just like every meal was worth the wait, so was the making of our home worth the wait.

The beautiful color of the tan panel and white floor tiles had a very rich look. The mirrored glass on the back wall of our living room. gave it a look of elegance. One would never have believed its appearance from when we first saw it. Truly as scripture records in 2 Corinthians 5:17 that old things are passed away; behold, all things are become new.

We saw a complete transformation and I remember thinking, "We're about to be living in style!" One thing I liked about our home was having my own room, then one day, my answered prayer baby sister moved in with me.

Yes, she was the blessing I had prayed for, and like any other sibling she got into my stuff. I called myself having a hiding place for my things only I could enjoy. Thin Mints was my favorite cookie treat whether store-bought or from the Girl Scouts. Soon enough I found out little sis liked them too!

SIBLING LOVE IS AN UNBREAKABLE THREAD WOVEN INTO THE FABRIC OF MY LIFE.
-AFFIRM

Chapter 6: A Prayer Reminder

As time passed, my sister and I became true siblings. Loving each other one day, and not-so-much the next. When she was born my very thought was that I would never hurt her nor let anyone else hurt her. Then one day I had to eat those words.

I'd come home from a very hard school day and only my Thin Mints would soothe my not-so-friendly mood. Running straight to my room, and opening my top drawer under my favorite PJs, I could smell chocolate before I saw the half-closed box. Then as I completely opened what had been a half-full box with only one treat left for me, I screamed so loud, "L—I—S—A!!!!!"

My mother answered, "She is outside playing. Before you go to bed tonight I want the room cleaned."

I cried trying to tell Mom how little sister had eaten my mints. I was so mad I told Mother, I was going to get her and when I did she won't touch anything else of mind. Mother laughed and told me she would handle it and reminded me saying, "You prayed for her and now she's here, your own special little baby doll."

Then with a kind of grin, Mom said, "Well you got her and she's growing up. At each stage of her life always remember God answered your prayer." And of course, as it's said, Mom added, "This too will pass."

When baby sister came in the house later, my mind had not changed, and before I knew it, I had laid hands.

We slept in bunk beds and she actually had the higher one. With her foot dangling down over the side of her bed, I snatched her leg, and down she came with a thump. Her screaming was painful to my ears, but not nearly as painful as my backside was when Mother got done with me. Why couldn't she use a belt like other moms? The extension cord left scars.

Lisa was the victim cradled and rocked in Mom's arms while I headed to the refrigerator to get ice for the knot on her head. I felt awful. Then I heard Mother say, "Is this why you asked for a sister? Is it? Is it?"

My pain worsened. Baby sister apologized and I accepted her words with a hug and a kiss that healed my hurt... and just like that we were friends again.

And I found a new hiding place for my treats.

-Reflections of My Family Treasures-

OUR CONNECTION REMINDS ME THAT I AM NEVER ALONE ON THIS JOURNEY.
-AFFIRM

Chapter 7: Big Brother Jimmy

I was proud to have an older brother, When people bothered me or called me names, I would always say, "I'm gonna tell my big brother."

For the most part, we were great siblings as we followed Mom's instructions. But when we didn't, my oldest sibling and I seemed to always be at it. We didn't like when Mother left him in charge, which was always going to be since he was the oldest.

Jimmy always wanted to do things his way and not like Mom had said. My mother worked two jobs. She served the Johnstown Police Department as a meter maid from 9 to 5 p.m. Dressed in those beautiful blue suits, hair pulled back and her cap, I thought she was the most beautiful woman ever, my mom. In the evenings she worked at the Sanitary Dairy packing ice cream.

I missed it when she wasn't home. Mom would say, "No company while I'm away. You have sisters you need to take care of and protect."

Brother had other things on his mind. His friends came and he let them in while the rest of us siblings repeatedly warned him about what Mom said.

We would run and hide, locking our bedroom doors, as his friends echoed behind our brother, "Get up those steps!" Our main threat which was always our comeback, "You wait till Mom get home."

But, as always, we were asleep when Mother came home, and before we knew it, we were waking to a brand new day and time for school. We never got to tell on Jimmy and every Friday, it was the same old thing. I felt like something needed to be done.

Truth is I didn't want to be the bad guy squealing on him. I also knew Mom expected him to follow her words. I knew I would still love him even though he did contrary to the rules and figured I would handle it.

I, being the oldest girl, felt like I could help set him straight. I was three years younger. I watched Mighty Mouse and I believed if he could save the day, so could I. My mind became full of ways to set Big Brother straight. Then one day my imagination became reality.

I had closed my mind to all mother's advice—to love, be thankful, and forgive. I tried to reason with him, but he wasn't hearing me. He just kept reminding me that he was the oldest as he laughed.

This was going to be harder than I thought.

I AM OPEN TO NURTURING AND GROWING OUR SIBLING BOND EVEN FURTHER.

-AFFIRM

Chapter 8: Fed Up and Tired

From habits recognized early on, we realized we had to take care of ourselves while Mother worked. In school, I was a runner. Track and field was my specialty. I was pretty good and proud of it.

I remember one day being pushed down by my older sibling. He was quick, too. However, on this occasion, I jumped up off the floor, grabbed a hard plastic cereal bowl and ran to the door.

Jimmy was way up the street, taunting me and laughing as he kept coming close and then going further away. I remember he got close enough to my aim. I ran out and whirled that bowl up the street and made contact right upside his head. The bowl hit the ground cracking with blood on it and there was a look of shock, unbelief, and madness on Big Brother's face.

He came running at me with a vengeance. At that moment I remembered all of the skills my track coach taught me. As I breathed in and out looking straight ahead, I was chanting to myself, "Run, Theresa run," while gaining momentum.

He never did catch me and I was too afraid to go back home. Yet I was hoping he wasn't hurt too bad. I remember saying, "God please let him be ok." We had one rule that we all dreaded—if one of us children was out of order, the whole house suffered.

❦

Somehow, as it neared time for Mother to come home, we would become the perfect siblings. I remembered seeing Mother walking her last steps toward the house and I slipped through an open space between the fence and front porch, and sat there like a perfect angel. All was well for the moment.

Then I heard Mother say, "Jimmy where you get that knot from on your head?" Now I'd be in trouble because I had broken one of the pieces into a set of six. I left the room. I remembered thinking, "If he tells it, he's got to tell it all."

Mother never did ask me anything about it, however from time to time I'd hear her mention something about a cereal bowl missing. "I told y'all about eating all over the house. Check your rooms and find it," she'd say, "When I come home tonight, there better be six."

I wondered why she was so concerned about that hard plastic bowl. I didn't know it was Corelle dinnerware. Of course, the two of us knew the bowl was history, and since two wrongs never make a right, the subject stayed closed between us and our love grew.

-Reflections of My Family Treasures-

I never knew what he told Mom about the bump on his head. As the oldest siblings, we remembered Mom's steady teaching about loving and respecting one another.

❦

I loved taking pictures with my Polaroid. One day while the other siblings and I were doing all kinds of poses, Jimmy said, "Hey sis, let's get a pic together." I was shocked and said, "Do you mean it?"

I thought he was going to prank me because of the bowl incident, and said so. Then a major moment I'll never forget occurred as he spoke these words "I wouldn't hurt you for the world, sis, nor let anybody else harm you. I'll always be the oldest and I'll always love you."

With that being said and sealed by a hug, one of the siblings snapped the best picture Jimmy and I ever took. I knew I would treasure his words always. Despite our sibling rivalry, true love walked among us and we were able to say we were sorry about our unwise decisions, forgiving one another and moving forward. Thank you, Big Brother.

—Reflections of My Family Treasures—

SIBLING LOVE FILLS MY HEART WITH WARMTH, UNDERSTANDING, AND COMPASSION.

-AFFIRM

BL*CKSEEDSPUBLISHING.
PLANTING SEEDS OF LOVE, FORGIVENESS & HEALING

Chapter 9: A Welcomed Addition

Family is the greatest thing. Now that I had been blessed with my little sister, Mother could have all the boys she wanted; and she did.

First came Timothy. We called him Timmy. As memory serves me, he was a scrawny little long baby and not so cute. I often thought Mom came home with the wrong baby. I personally nicknamed him ugly speaking under my breath.

After being taught to be thankful for one another, I would never want Mom to hear me say that out loud. I was not a good big sister at the time. I remember pounding him extra hard when the burping time came. I'd say, "I'll burp him." He drank milk faster than any of the kids before him.

It took a while to know that Timmy was sickly. After Mother made several trips to the doctor, she always came back home with him until the time she didn't. Mom was sad, and that made me sad too.

She said he needed tests and then he'd be home. Seeing his empty bassinet didn't help me at all. I began to regret the way I had treated him. When tears began to fall I felt ashamed, I promised myself and God I'd do better by him from now on. I prayed for the Lord to forgive me.

When Mom finally came home with him, I was so glad to see him and ready to be a big sister. Burping time became more meaningful. He made the funniest expressions when the big belch came, and I smiled and gave him a big kiss.

My funniest memory of Timmy was his childhood Easter speech. He couldn't get past the first line because people thought he was being smart. Laughter kept filling the sanctuary.

Finally, he blurted out, "What are you looking at me for, I didn't come to stay. I just came to wish you a Happy Easter day!" I remembered clapping so hard for him.

He actually grew up to be quite handsome and loving, playing basketball for Greater Johnstown High Trojans. He was in all the Christmas tournaments at the Johnstown War Memorial.

Tim was good at hitting those baskets far and near. When he graduated High school, I was so proud of him as the family and I cheered him on, "Go Tim!"

I watched him grow into a very loving brother who cared about his siblings, especially his sisters. His actions spoke louder than words, if he said he was going do something or be there, you could count on Tim.

I remember him cleaning my shoes for one Easter Sunday. We all couldn't get new ones. Tim assured me of how good they would look as he was going to shine them up and they did. I walked proudly down the street to the church. More than the look of my pretty shoes, I smiled because of the good deed my brother had fulfilled. Thank you, my dependable loving brother.

WE CELEBRATE EACH OTHER'S SUCCESSES AND PROVIDE COMFORT DURING CHALLENGES.
-AFFIRM

Chapter 10: Then Came Keith

Our number 7th sibling arrived, in 1972 on a hot July day. A boy of all boys—Keith Allen McNair would be the comedian of the family. As he grew, he kept us all in stitches.

Our older brother Jimmy, now grown and serious about his steady Roxanne, made it plain that he didn't care what we thought about her, she was his God-given gift. He was gonna marry Roxanne.

They were married and moved into a blue-shingled house on the street behind us. We loved our sister-in-law. With Jimmy out of the house, I was the next oldest sibling in charge.

Watching Keith was not an easy task. He was slick. You couldn't catch him and the faces he made were hilarious. We'd end up laughing so hard before we knew it, he was gone.

The funniest thing I remember about Keith is that he loved Oreo cookies. Mom loved them too. After a long day at work, she would like to relax with a cold glass of milk and her cookies. She had her own special hiding place in a drawer in her bedroom.

All I remember is she came home really tired after her first job. Her feet were tired from checking meters all day and she couldn't wait to get off of them. Saying hello to us, she climbed those 15 steps to the second floor, telling us to wake her up by six. The next sound we heard was this shrill scream, "Who been in my room and where's my cookies?!"

You've probably guessed it already. Down the steps, she came with a vengeance. One thing we knew was not to touch her stuff, especially her Oreos. We were all scared because everybody would be punished until the truth was known. It just so happened that Keith wasn't home and by the time Mom finished drilling us, it was time for her second job.

She wasn't happy as she eyed us all saying, "When I come in tonight," and then added her favorite saying, "somebody's gonna tell me something." With those words, she was gone and we all had one name in our thoughts— Keith.

He bounced in not knowing what any of the rest of us had been through. He denied any part of eating Mom's cookies and was asleep when she got home late that night.

But early the next morning I remember awakening to Mom giving him the shakedown. I awoke hearing her say, "I'm gonna ask you one more time, did you eat my cookies?"

Keith said, "No Mom no," and immediately his face broke out all over in the shape of an Oreo. If I hadn't seen it myself, I wouldn't have believed it.

Mom shoved him to the mirror where he could see his reflection. He couldn't deny it any longer, and of course, he said, "I'm sorry," with a hung head. Right then, right there, I made sure I didn't go anywhere near Mom's treats.

Well, I was getting over eating all of the lemon meringue and leaving an empty pie shell—the many whoopings I got about doing it. But after Keith's episode, I was afraid that pie would tell on me. In short, my funny baby brother's habit helped heal mine. Thank you, Brother.

―Reflections of My Family Treasures―

I AM A SOURCE OF LOVE, ENCOURAGEMENT, AND INSPIRATION FOR MY SIBLINGS.

-AFFIRM

Chapter 11: Life in the Big House

I recognized right away that owning your own home was better than renting. $1.00 had been paid for our big house, which was fast becoming a home. We took pride in our parent's hard labor and work, some days from sun up til late evenings. When we went to school they were working and when we came home, we could smell the best smell ever.

While Jay continued working on the outside of our beautiful newly painted house, Mother prepared hot biscuits and a pot of beef stew. The only thing we all noticed was the fact that the big house was becoming smaller. We were growing. The boys were getting longer legs. We needed more drawer and closet space.

Life in Kernville had been okay so far. We had a lot of bumps bruises aggravation and happiness, I recalled as well. I was also outgrowing my siblings as my interest was changing. Home is the sweetest word in the English dictionary. We had everything we needed. Clothes and shoes are fresh and clean, not always if ever the top brands. Mom kept us looking good.

I remember when she got an increase in her pay. Mother had a J.C. Penny account and took me shopping. Mom's night job at the Sanitary Dairy went from five nights to two nights. Mother was home more which I loved. She spoke of meeting ends cause less money was coming in.

Mother was smart, she used her skills of cooking to work. She and Jay scheduled a fish fry two Fridays a month. The house was full. We passed out the flyers far and wide, hitting every street. The couples would hold each other and lights low, which was our signal to go upstairs.

Of course, I would sneak down and get an eyeful of as much as I could. Then one day I heard a sound. A familiar sound. It was the slamming of an old back door.

Across the alley, a big family was moving into the double house adjacent to us. I could see quite a few girls and then noticed three guys, one of whom particularly caught my eye. My emotions within went wild. My legs were knocking, hands sweating. I remember thinking, "Wow he's gorgeous, what a cutie!"

Images of someone holding me tight like the couples at the fish fry flooded my mind. Life was just about to get a lot more interesting. Now I had more on my mind than siblings and school. I was now occupied with knowing the new kids next door. One in particular.

OUR UNIQUE PERSONALITIES COMPLEMENT EACH OTHER, CREATING A HARMONIOUS BOND.
-AFFIRM

Chapter 12: A New Attitude

In the following days, I could think of nothing else except my future husband. There's a common saying in the church world to 'name it and claim it' and that became my mindset. I just knew he was it!

I hadn't had a chance to meet any of them, but when the weekend was over while walking up the alley that divided our homes, there he was in his window. I remember speaking and he said nothing.

One day one of the boys I liked walked me home from school, and there he was in the window. The next time I came home by myself, he spoke. "Hey girl."

I said, "Oh, you can talk."

He said, "I see you and your little crossed-eyed boyfriend holding your books."

I told him to mind his business. After that, I was always looking forward to seeing him and disappointed when he wasn't there.

Finally, I learned his name by hearing one of his siblings call him. I looked to see which brother would answer. "Jimbo, Mom wants you," she called.

Now I had a name to go with that cute face. That name melted my heart, and of course, I couldn't wait to say his name to him. So the very next time he was in his window as I came home from school, he yelled, "Hey skinny girl!" I responded, calling him by his name.

"Who told you my name, what's yours?" He asked.

I replied, "Not skinny girl."

He had a slingshot and aimed a rock toward me, but this skinny girl could run. From then on it was always a tease between him and me.

Finally, he would be outside when school was over. He would say something and if I didn't reply, he would run and catch me with a punch to the arm. He was fast too.

Well, our relationship grew to where he would come over to the house. He loved my mom and the three of us would play cards until Mom would yawn, and it was time for him to go.

His family had dogs and you could hear him whistling for them. We formed our own signal late at night after he would get in from band practice, he would whistle once for the dogs and three times for me and I would go up to the bathroom window where we talked for hours. Even though there were two or three houses within earshot, we didn't care that they could hear us, for love had turned the corner.

The sounds of cars passing by drowned out a lot of our conversation. I was all of 15 years old. Jimbo was two years older and about to soon graduate. As we got to know each other I found that his plans would take him away from Johnstown for a while. He planned to join the Coast Guard after school.

Before meeting Jim as I came to call him, I had already planned to go to Greater Johnstown High School. The city had plans for a new school, which caused busing. Greater Johnstown Vocational Technical School, what a beautiful layout. Jim was going there and so was I, singing my happy song, Wherever he goes I go.

-Reflections of My Family Treasures-

SIBLING LOVE TEACHES ME VALUABLE LESSONS ABOUT PATIENCE AND COMPROMISE.
-AFFIRM

Chapter 13: Rise and Shine

For the next two years, Monday through Friday brought an early rise. We needed to be at the bus stop by 6:45 a.m. Getting up at 6:00 a.m. was hard, but we lived close to the stop.

As time would have it, Jim and I became an item and everybody seemed to know it. I was in love. Riding side-by-side to school together was sweet. We planned our hallway meetings all in the name of bathroom breaks. Lunch periods were nice and just knowing we were in the same building did my heart good.

As we grew closer so did our families. I made up my mind that I was going to marry this man. After school and our chores, we would end up playing board games and watching TV until it was time for him to go home. I can still hear Mom saying to us, "Y'all say your goodbyes in here." She was keeping an eye out for no hanky panky.

❦

However I was in love, and in the 11th grade, almost 16-years-old, knowing I should have listened... as I was a late bloomer. My cycle started at 14 years of age. I could still hear Jim saying, "My little sister is bigger than you," referring to the chest area.

I started feeling not-so-good in the mornings, and the rise and shine had risen and shown me that I was experiencing morning sickness. What's worse is that he was also experiencing being sick.

His mom knew right away. The many times she had yelled out the window, "Don't ya'll be doing what you shouldn't be doing." For a few moments of pleasure on that cement floor of my basement, what was I thinking?

Okay, I wasn't thinking... I was in love.

How many times in life had I heard the young ladies say, "It was only one time"? We only did it once. The only sure thing I knew was that my backside was never going to visit that cellar floor again.

So nervous and scared I found myself saying, "I'm sorry Lord." Jim's mother, a God-fearing woman, had schooled us concerning our behavior and I felt like I owed her an apology, as well as the Lord.

-Reflections of My Family Treasures-

MY SIBLINGS ARE MY LIFELONG FRIENDS, AND OUR LOVE CONTINUES TO FLOURISH.
-AFFIRM

BLACKSEEDSPUBLISHING.
PLANTING SEEDS OF LOVE, FORGIVENESS & HEALING

Chapter 14: Reaping and Facing the Music

Have you heard of the proverb, what you sow you shall also reap? It simply means basically that how you treat people in life is how you will be treated. Or if you plant a seed on the unreceptive ground, you'll get an unreceptive product.

Even though there's a blessing in my reaping, I will never forget the day that Jim, father-to-be of our unborn child, came to tell my mother I was expecting.

> Be not deceived; God is not mocked: for whatsoever a man soweth, that shall he also reap. –Galatians 6:7

I was five months pregnant. I knew there would be repercussions and after he had been in the living room for a while, only silence filled the air. Suddenly, with a loud bellowing voice like a bass drum, I heard my name like I'd never heard it before. "TREE-SA!" Two syllables.

My body shook and I took off my glasses so I couldn't see her face. I tiptoed down the hallway making a slow entrance into our living room where Mother and Jim were sitting on the couch facing me.

Mother's first statement, "How many months did you say she is?" I was so small she could hardly believe her eyes. Then she said, "Come here." After feeling my tummy, she said, "Yep, you're pregnant." The next thing I know, I was at the doctors getting the vitamins for pregnant women, those big horse pills.

❦

The news was out and I still felt ashamed of my situation hearing Mom's echo of 'panties up and your dress down', but felt some relief because I didn't have to hide from Mom anymore. I remembered the story in the Bible of Jonah and the great fish. He didn't follow the Lord's instructions, and my disobedience to Mom was a reminder.

Like him, I hadn't listened either. God saved him from dangerous waters and Jim's intervention in speaking to Mom was my saving grace. She didn't say 'I told you so' or fuss at me. For that, I've always been so thankful. Also, to Jim for taking the responsibility in speaking to Mother on my behalf. A great big thanks to you, too!

With the big secret no longer before me, I remembered how my thoughts were to wait until I was married. In this season we both learned a great lesson—that Mother knows best. Hearing is good, but listening is far better.

Sixteen and expecting wasn't something I was proud of. Schoolwork, Co-op program, and housework was already a full-time job.

As the baby grew and I began to show, I was so ashamed because I had been schooled concerning this matter, but the deed had been done. There may have been many in the same situation, some excited and thrilled to show off their tummies, but not me.

One very comforting thing was having two loving mothers living next door to each other full of love and good advice. I needed all they had to give. They were about to become young grandmas early. Having this experience I would now instruct teenagers to wait, take your time, get your schooling, for love that is real will wait. For it is better to obey than to sacrifice.

1 Samuel 15:22 says:

> And Samuel said, Hath the Lord as great delight in burnt offerings and sacrifices, as in obeying the voice of the Lord? Behold, to obey is better than sacrifice, and to hearken than the fat of rams.

-Reflections of My Family Treasures-

I AM BLESSED TO EXPERIENCE THE BEAUTY OF SIBLING LOVE EVERY DAY.

-AFFIRM

BLCKSEEDSPUBLISHING.
PLANTING SEEDS OF LOVE, FORGIVENESS & HEALING

Chapter 15: Final Hurrah

Mother's favorite store for my clothes was the department store Sears. I loved their outfits for my little petite size. She found the most beautiful tops to make me comfortable and not show as much.

Off to the doctor for my vitamins. They were the biggest pills ever. I was able to go to school up to 7 and ½ months and then bed rest, feet up. My school work was sent home and I completed the 10th grade.

After a few appointments, the doctor determined I was too small to deliver my child and would need to have a C-section. I explained everything which was okay with me. I always dreaded what I knew and saw about mothers giving birth, having to push and blow, and the joyful scream, moan, or groan that came with delivering.

I was even given some dates to choose the birth of my child. The month of December was upon us. I asked for a Christmas baby. According to my time chart, the closest would be the 27th. I seemed more hungry than usual as the days got close.

One night I ate my last snack before bed. My favorite tasty food and drink, I found out later that I should not have mixed. Mom's collard greens and a cold glass of chocolate milk. "Yumm," I kept repeating until the very last taste of both.

Hours later around midnight, the stomach cramps were not-so-pleasant. We all thought that I was in labor. It was the 20th of December. After arriving at the hospital and a thorough examination, you guessed it, the diagnosis was gas. I made sure I never made that mistake again. Some things you just don't mix.

A week later, early in the morning of the 27th, I arrived at the hospital for the birth of my first child. Jim and my mom were right on the scene. With the name already prearranged as to it being a male or female, I awoke to a 6 pound, 19 ½ beautiful baby boy. Jimmie was here. I had a son.

Three days later with all the instructions on how to heal properly, I went home. The pain I experienced caused me to have one thought, which at the time I truly meant. "I'm never doing this again."

Only time will tell. One thing however great the pain, when I looked at what God had allowed me to bring into this world, a smile and fast-beating heart would occur. I was nervous having stepped into an adult situation, knowing I had a lot of play in me. I was now a mom, all of 16-years-old, with a healthy fine son. I prayed, "Lord forgive me for being disobedient to Mom's rules." I could hear her still saying in the back of my mind, "Keep your panties up and your dress down."

Only God knew what paths and roads were before us, and which ones we would take. As for now, Jimmie was my newest family jewel, and as he grew, I would teach him all that Mother had taught us about healing love, thankfulness, and forgiveness... and I believed the Lord would help me.

Job 23:10 says:

> But he knoweth the way that I take: when he hath tried me, I shall come forth as gold.

WE CELEBRATE EACH OTHER'S SUCCESSES AND PROVIDE COMFORT DURING CHALLENGES.
-AFFIRM

Chapter 16: Kudos to You Mom

I n this closing chapter of my story, I sing Hallelujah the highest praise, for a mother that kept us on track by sticking to her word.

We soon learned that whether she spoke encouragement of what we would receive for behaving or the punishment for not behaving, Mother said what she meant and meant what she said.

We grew up in the 60's and 70's, far different from today where kids talk back or tell their parents what to do. We learned that if we said anything at all, it had better be so low under our breath that we nearly choked trying to say it.

We learned to sit still, stop tapping on the table, stop whistling, and move when Mom said move. I'm reminded of all the great results Mother's instructions provided, when we listened, and the not-so-great when we didn't. 'I'll do it later' or 'in a few minutes' wasn't in our vocabulary. After a few attempts to do it our way, we found out it wasn't worth it.

Sometimes we learn the hard way. I remember Big Brother liked to tap with pencils on the tabletop. Mom had said a few times to stop, and finally, she said, "Tap again and I'm gonna knock your head off." After a quiet moment, he did it again. Mom was on him so quick for not doing what she had said, thank goodness, but the tapping ceased.

We learned not to make Mom waste her breath saying the same thing twice. The punishments made us wish we had just yielded the first time. If you were given a week with no television, you'd better not be caught coming downstairs for milk two and three times. Mom caught on to that trick quick. We just added days to the already jail time.

Even our pastor said she was a no-nonsense woman at Mom's home going. The days of yesteryear gave us good instructions from a loving mother. All we had to do was hear and obey it. Being the eldest gave us responsibilities we didn't ask for, or want to do. As young siblings, we learned early how to help each other as well as the twins, who were only crib babies. We changed their diapers, and fed formula to them.

For me, the thrill was gone. After being caught and punished, I was no longer hooked on formula. Mother had a way of explaining our wrongs that made us feel so sorry even though it was true. She'd say, "Bottled milk is the only food your brothers can digest right now. They need every ounce of milk to grow. You are big enough to eat table food, so if you drink their milk what will they have?"

Mom's words caused me to think deeply. I didn't want to be the cause of stunting their growth. Maturity causes you to look back on life and say 'I should have known better'.

I particularly learned that Mother knows best. I had been told never to mess with the washing machine. Thrilled to see how the water was squeezed out through those wooden rollers made me curious. Trying to put something that I thought wouldn't take long so as not to get caught, was a big mistake. I was too short to begin with and the baby doll's shoe was so small. Before I knew it, the shoe was grabbed and my hand too. Obedience is better than sacrifice.

❦

Knowing the Lord now as I do in my senior years, I think twice before I say or do. It's an automatic reaction. I learned to pray believing, doubting nothing, and certain the Lord would answer my prayers because my mother told me He's able—and that was good enough for me as a child.

One thing particularly we all learned as the siblings began to grow up, is the old adage, that a family that prays together, stays together. Together became a household name in our home. Even though we all had different chores to do, the bigger ones were always done first.

Rather than hurry the others because no one could go out until all was done, we learned to help each other as a team. The chores were done in no time at all.

Mother had borne seven of us living. She instilled in us that we had each other and never to say we didn't have anyone to play with us. Mother made sure we had all the sports equipment our yard could hold. We learned to bandage each other's cuts and bruises, run to get ice for our bumps when we fell and kiss the boo-boo.

The greatest lesson of all we learned is that together we can make it. Our parents worked hard and bought us what they could afford. We learned to appreciate what they blessed us with in clothes and shoes. We wouldn't have known there were shoes called bo bo's if it hadn't crossed our ear gate. We were very thankful for all we received in food, clothes, shelter, and one another. We were rich in ways we knew not.

Family, true treasures living under one roof. Every talk session Mother gave us about how, when, and what to do, even the why, we now instruct our own children and grandchildren. As I watch them hug each other and say 'I'm sorry', I see continual healing love built upon thanksgiving and forgiveness.

-Reflections of My Family Treasures-

> ## *"FAMILY IS NOT AN IMPORTANT THING. IT'S EVERYTHING."*
> – MICHAEL J. FOX

BLCKSEEDSPUBLISHING.
PLANTING SEEDS OF LOVE, FORGIVENESS & HEALING

Special Tribute to Siblings

Below are tributes to my siblings and their loving families.

Siblings may come and siblings may go
But there's one thing we will always know
Mother taught us real truths on how to survive
So our sibling love would always thrive
Down through the years our loves grown strong
No need to argue about who's right or wrong
For we learned that a soft answer drives away wrath
Therefore, keeping with joy, forgiveness in our path.

I'm so proud of each and every one of you my siblings, for keeping family values and instilling them in our children, as they will instill them in theirs.

-Reflections of My Family Treasures-

James Albert Myers Jr.

My oldest sibling Jimmy
Born first of our crew
The head of our sibling ship
As one by one we grew

Theresa Ann Myers-Jones

Blessed to be the second born
And first girl of the crowd
I took my place as sibling two
Small stature with voice so loud

Derrick Myers

Because He came out first
That made him sibling three
A mindset lifted to the gospel
His heart set for victory

Frederick Myers

Then came Fred after his twin
A bit smaller and a bit thin
Though not identical they did favor
He stuck to his word, never to waver

–Reflections of My Family Treasures–

Lisa Michele Myers-Graves
My little sister in which I prayed
Lord, send a baby girl my way
The lord heard me and blessed me he did
With a strong sibling soul who grew also to pray

Reggie Myers
Born a special gift on my fathers side
The love of God in him did abide
He loved to strum his guitar and sing
Oh the joy to our hearts he'd bring

Darla Renee Myers
With fourteen years between us
We were ever so very close
She was always lifting a helping hand
To give big sister her most

Timothy Dwayne McNair
I call him the brother of champions
Who grew up with a caring heart
To love his family unconditionally
Which God gave him to do from the very start

Keith Allen McNair
Oh, my baby brother Keith
Born last of the Flock
Kept us laughing in stitches
All around the clock

-Reflections of My Family Treasures-

CONTINUED TRIBUTES

Jimmy our oldest sibling married Roxanne and blessed us with two sons and three daughters
Derrick married Karen and blessed us with a daughter
Fred blessed us with two sons
Lisa married Mark and blessed us with a son and four daughters
Timothy married Nicole, blessing us with three sons, total four sons
Keith blessed us with a son and three daughters
I married Jim and blessed us with two sons and two daughters
Treasures, treasures, treasures and the training continues on with
The Arrival of my first jewel
Jimmie Jr.
The first seed of my womb
Born to plant in this world
Showing love, respect and honesty
To each sibling boy and girl

My desired take away from my story would be that siblings as they grow together would come to know who and what their siblings are about as we can encourage each other and push one another towards the greatness in them.

Always remember that we are a part of each other, a jewel from our mother's womb and father's love. If we keep love in the fore front of our circumstances and situations no matter how great or small they may be, the power of forgiveness with thanksgiving will flow as healing keeps our peaceful unity united.

My prayer is that every reader or listener of my reflected memories will grasp the wisdom of how wonderful life can be when you have a sibling who loves, cares and respects you as you do them.

Finally knowing that the power of love can have great effects, I'm reminded of the Lord Jesus command in John 13:34:

> A new commandment I give unto you, That ye love one another; as I have loved you, that ye also love one another.

If you're feeling the void of a sibling, and you miss them, yet they are the one whom you feel broke the bond and pride is slowing you down from making the mend, Pray this prayer with me:

"Dear God, help me. I can not do this on my own. I miss my sibling yet I long to make things right. Lord open my mouth and give me what and how to say that which needs to be spoken to open this door. You are the Author of Love. As You walk with me I know that forgiveness and thanksgiving will spill over causing the past to flee, as healing with joy will start the next chapter of our loving sibling relationship. Amen"

God bless your new family treasure.

🌱 🌱 🌱

It gives me great honor to share some of my family portraits with you on the following pages.

-Reflections of My Family Treasures-
Family Treasures

Siblings
Timmy, Theresa, & Keith

Siblings
Lisa & Theresa

Brother Fred
& Granddaughters

Son Jimmie, Theresa,
Siblings Derrick & Darla

Son
Jimmie

Sister
Lisa

About the Author

Hey there, I'm Theresa A. Jones, and I come from the charming city of Johnstown, Pa. I'm happily married to Elder Joseph Jones, and together, we're proud parents—mother and stepfather—to four wonderful kids: Jimmie Jr., Tiffany, Tonya, and Justin. Oh, and I can't forget to mention that I'm a super proud grandma to 17 amazing grandkids and even have a great grandson in the mix! How wonderful, right?

Now, I wear a few hats in life. I'm not just a grandma and a wife, I'm also a Television Evangelist, an ordained pastor, and a visionary. But that's not all—I've got a creative side too! I absolutely love writing poetry, short stories, and those heartwarming greeting cards that make people smile.

My journey with faith has been quite the ride. Back in 1992, I got my Evangelist license from Ark Ministry International. That's where I met Bishop James D. Dillingham Jr. and First Lady Lynn. They're like a rock-solid foundation for me, and my faith and love in Christ only grew stronger from there.

Here's a cool highlight: in December 1995, I had this incredible vision. It led me to start Power Unlimited TV Ministry. It's a way to reach out to those who can't easily get out and about—like shut-ins. For 28 years now, this outreach has been airing at 5:00 pm in Johnstown and its surrounding areas. What an amazing journey it's been!

Fast forward to 2006, when I was attending the Church of God In Christ. Elder Robert T Scholfield's teachings really resonated with me, and that's when I had this new vision. This time, it was for something called a Rescue Station—a way to help more of God's people.

The Rescue Station dream became a reality in my living room, and thus, Abundant Life Ministry House of Prayer was born. I'm so thrilled to be serving as the Senior Pastor, and we're now in our 16th year of making a difference. Our church family just keeps growing, and it's incredible to see how God's word continues to touch lives.

And guess what? People are at the core of everything I do. Aside from being a mom, grandma, and pastor, I also get to spend a few days a week in a religious setting at a local thrift store. It's such a rewarding experience to connect with folks, offer a friendly smile, and spread hope and peace. The best part is, I get just as much as I give.

Now, when it comes to my written works, I've been fortunate enough to have some of my pieces published. There's a touching poem called "A Cry from the Womb," a heartfelt piece called "Congratulations Class of 2020," and I even have a book chapter titled "The Treasures of My Unlocked Heart."

I'm so thankful for all the beautiful experiences and opportunities in my life. Each day, I find myself thanking God for the incredible journey, especially for Abundant Life Ministry House of Prayer—a true Rescue Station for God's people. People are the heart of my story, and it's a joy to share a smile, offer hope, and spread peace wherever I go.

Acknowledgements

Special thanks go out to my Lord and Savior for the incredible gift of writing. My heartfelt gratitude to my husband Joseph, my daughters Tiffany Hardison and Tonya McClurkin, as well as my sister and dear friend Elder Lisa Graves. I'm also thankful for my niece and author Elder Sarina Hardison, my friend and fellow author Evangelist Debra Bush, and Black Seeds Publishing.

Their unwavering encouragement has inspired me to wield the pen, always reminding me that I can conquer anything through Christ who empowers me (Phil. 4:13, KJV). And to my 17 wonderful grandchildren—Tamia, Jimorie, Tanajea, Raymond, Savasia, Ramiya, Jimiere, Samiyah, Keyland, Javon-JJ, LeDavien, Jordan, Lelanii, Ay'Lynn, AlleVeon, Ariella, and AuGuste—you're learning the vital lessons of love, respect, forgiveness, and gratitude, and you fill my heart with immeasurable joy.

-Reflections of My Family Treasures-

THE END

In the next edition of my autobiography part 2, life's lessons continue as my journey broadens and maturity flourishes.

Now…
It's your chance to write your OWN Reflections >>>

-Reflections of My Family Treasures-

MY FAMILY TREASURE REFLECTIONS

-Reflections of My Family Treasures-

-Reflections of My Family Treasures-

www.ingramcontent.com/pod-product-compliance
Lightning Source LLC
Chambersburg PA
CBHW021319110426
42743CB00049B/3421